Confessions of a Church Mouse

Confessions of a Church Mouse

There's one in every Congregation

Bre'nae Whiteley

© 2018 Bre'nae Whiteley
All rights reserved.

ISBN-13: 9780997385601
ISBN-10: 099738560X
Library of Congress Control Number: 2016906402
Bre'nae Whiteley, Carrollton, TX

*Because He has inclined His ear unto me,
Therefore, I will call upon Him,
For as long as I shall live.*

—Psalms 116:2

To Alvetta King-Bell, I did not have the opportunity to talk to you about this project, but I am in no way surprised to learn that to your family, friends, and fellow congregation members, you were known as a great intercessor, getting up to be at 5:00 a.m. prayer service. I take great comfort in knowing that you are still standing in the gap, looking down, and watching over us. We love and miss you very much.

To my family, I love you all. I pray that God continues to work with us, on us, and through us.

To:

_____.

From:

_____.

*Prayer is the most powerful action against trials,
the most effective medicine against sickness,
and the most valuable gift we can give to someone
we love or care for.*

Preface

While standing in a circle in the fellowship hall prior to entering the choir stand, the choir was getting ready to consecrate. As always, the choir president asked if someone would say a prayer. Normally, this is where everyone looks around at each other, but this time, before anyone could respond, a fellow choir member commented, "Sis Whiteley doesn't pray." I will say it caught me off guard a little; however, at that moment, I realized that if you are not the person always standing up in front of the church speaking, making announcements, praying loudly, or leading worship service, to some it means that you are not living a prayer-filled life. Don't get me wrong; they may never tell you this face-to-face. Remember, we are in church. However, I realized that many Christians and fellow members had come to this same conclusion.

I began to think about several of my fellow members, many of them, much like me, quiet, dont say a lot, they are not the center of attention. perhaps the same opinions have been formed about them. Who are we to question someone else's prayer life? We should only examine our own. If you were to ask me, in my opinion, all churches could do with a few more members who do more listening than speaking anyway.

We may not be down front leading a long, drawn-out prayer, but this does not mean we don't live a prayer-filled life. In my opinion, prayer is actually more important than going to church, and I consider going to church very important. With that said, I would never lead a prayer for the approval of others, and I am not afraid of leading a prayer for fear of disapproval.

Before I go any further, let me say that I don't consider myself a teacher, a minister, or an evangelist—or a writer. I'm just that quiet member at the back of the church. So if I must be lumped into a category, then like many of my fellow quiet Christians, put me in the category of "the church mouse." Every congregation has them.

This book is a result of my own quiet, personal journey to strengthen my communication with God and to establish a better understanding of prayer, its purpose, and its effects on my personal journey. The goal of this mouse is to learn to communicate more effectively with God. I invite you all on this journey with me. I pray that you will accept this challenge, get involved, and participate in this exercise.

Contents

I	Childhood Prayer and Tradition	1
II	To Pray without Ceasing	3
III	What Is Our Motive for Praying?	7
IV	The Types of Prayer	9
V	Understanding the Lord's Prayer	24
VI	Examples of Prayer	28
VII	Confessions of a Church Mouse Prayer Journal	39
	Journal Examples:	43
	About the Author	75
	Recommended Reading	77

I
Childhood Prayer and Tradition

When I was younger, adults would say, "She is as quiet as a church mouse." I always wondered where that saying came from. Aren't we supposed to be quiet in church? That's what I was taught: go to church, be quiet, listen, and learn. Don't misunderstand me; praise and worship are very important. After all, I sing in the choir. It is my job to minister through song, to witness to the gospel, and more important, to listen.

Now I understand the peaceful life of the church mouse a little bit better. Like the church mouse, I want to be fed and be allowed to scurry back to a warm spot to reflect on the day's lesson. I'm not concerned with being seen, and I don't need the spotlight. I just want the message that the Lord has sent to me through His messenger. Although the pews are filled every Sunday, I believe that every message that the pastor delivers is really a secret-coded message just for me from God. So I quietly take my seat, take as many notes as I can, then, I hurry home to reflect on the message, trying to decipher what my message from God is on this particular Wednesday or Sunday.

One Sunday, after returning home from service, my thoughts turned to prayer—not just the thought of praying but how I prayed. Yes, I know that everyone can pray, but are my prayers working in concert with God? Am I effective in my communication with God? This reminded me of something that I had heard over the years, and I honestly can't remember where I was the first time I heard it. I remember hearing it said more than once. "Some of us are just wasting our time praying because our prayers are just going up, hitting the ceiling, and coming back down." This troubled me. Why? What would cause my prayers to hit the ceiling, so to speak, and come back down? So I sat down and started to take a close inventory of how and when I communicated with God. I realized that as a child, I learned the child's prayer Now I Lay Me Down to Sleep, and when I became a preteen or teenager, I was taught the Lord's Prayer ("Our Father who art in heaven…"). But as I sat there reflecting, I could not remember ever being taught the specific types of prayer, their purpose, and how to effectively pray. Don't get me wrong; I was taught that it is important to pray. I was taught that it is more important for me to talk to God than for God to talk to me. Every church and every pastor teaches that we are to pray without ceasing (1 Thess. 5:17). But I was not taught the specifics of prayer. Imagine my surprise at this revelation. I had been going to church for years, but I could not put my finger on the time when I actually sat through a lesson on prayer. Please understand again that I am not saying that my pastor never taught his congregation about prayer. He has certainly had lessons on prayer and the importance of prayer. I am saying that I could not remember being taught all the different types of prayers and the significance of each of them. Maybe I was absent that Wednesday night of Bible study, or maybe I missed all of that during the time I was in my twenties, hanging out, not attending anyone's church on a regular basis. I'm not sure when or how I missed that part of the lesson, but I knew that this was where I had to start. After all, 2 Timothy 2:15 states, "Study to shew thyself approved unto God, a workman that needeth not to be ashamed, rightly dividing the word of truth."

The rendering "study to show thyself approved unto God" is only found in the King James Version, translated in the year 1611. In 1611, the word "study" meant to strive or be diligent. If I were to communicate effectively with God, I would have to be diligent. It would involve much study, contemplation, and prayer. It would involve bringing an open mind, an open heart, and a faithful life to the word of truth.

II

To Pray without Ceasing

What does that mean? 1 Thessalonians 5:16–18 states, "Rejoice evermore, Pray without ceasing, in everything give thanks: for this is the will of God in Christ Jesus concerning you." "Without ceasing" means continuously, so that means we are to pray continuously.

Well, I had to stop right there because if I am honest, my first confession is that I had already miserably fallen short of this request from God. Yes, I prayed, but my first confession is that I also ceased.

In the mornings, I would get up and say, "Thank you, Lord, for another day." I went about my daily routine, making coffee, getting breakfast, getting dressed, making sure Mom was set for the day, heading out to my office, and so on. Did I miss other opportunities to pray during my morning routine? Had my prayer life also become a victim of this Shake and Bake microwave society we live in? Was I so busy that I couldn't pray without ceasing? I had to ask myself these questions.

I am reminded of a morning prayer I once read on the Internet: "So far today, God, I've done all things right. I haven't gossiped, lost my temper, or been greedy, grumpy, nasty, selfish, or overindulgent. I'm very thankful for that, but in a few minutes, God, I am going to get out of bed, and from then on I am probably going to need a lot more help."

Amen.

I realized that though I had thanked God for allowing me to see another day, my feet had just hit the floor. If I wanted to be under the cover of prayer all day, I had to take advantage of every opportunity to pray as it presented itself throughout my day.

If we are praying without ceasing, that means we are praying while we are making coffee, making breakfast, washing dishes, driving, changing the baby, or running the lawn mower. With the daily demands of our busy lives, we can't always be on our knees, so how do we pray continuously? I must confess, the answer is that we don't, for a few simple reasons.

Most often, we fail to pray without ceasing because we confine our prayers to a place and a time. I am reminded of the story in John 4:20–24 when the woman at the well asked Jesus whether Samaria or Jerusalem was the true place of worship.

> Our fathers worshiped in this mountain; and ye say, that in Jerusalem is the place where men ought to worship.
>
> Jesus saith unto her, Woman, believe me, the hour cometh when ye shall neither in this mountain nor yet at Jerusalem, worship the Father.
>
> Ye worship ye know not what: we know what we worship: for salvation is of the Jews.
>
> But the hour cometh and now is when the true worshipers shall worship the Father in spirit and in truth: for the Father seeketh such to worship him.
>
> God is a Spirit: and they that worship Him must worship Him in spirit and in truth.
>
> God in His infinite perfection is everywhere at the same time so His worship would no longer be confined to a place or form, but Spiritual as God Himself is Spiritual.

Understand that while it is important to have a prayer closet or war room (a private place to go and pray), in Matthew 6:6 the bible tells us, "When you pray, enter into your closet, and when you have shut your door, pray to your Father who is in secret, and your Father who sees in secret shall reward you openly." If we are to pray without ceasing, our prayers cannot be confined to just these spaces.

In order to accomplish our goal of praying without ceasing, we must first always be "online" with God, so when the Holy Spirit moves us to pray, we can instantly agree with Him. Part of the answer is found in 1 Thessalonians 5:16 and 18. Here it describes to us how to be online with God in order to maintain healthy communication with the Lord.

Verse 16: Rejoice Evermore. We must maintain an attitude of Joyfulness,

Verse 18: In everything give thanks: for this is the will of God in Christ Jesus concerning you.

We must maintain a mental attitude of thankfulness.

Romans 8:26 states, "Likewise the Spirit also helpeth our infirmities: for we know not what we should pray for as we ought: but the Spirit itself maketh intercession for us, with the groanings which cannot be uttered."

This means that the Holy Spirit carries our messages to God. What this scripture is telling us is that the feelings and enticements of our hearts are also understood through the Holy Spirit and not just our words. If we are online with God, it is possible to pray without ceasing because the Holy Spirit will carry those feelings that we have to God even though we are not able to put those feelings or enticements into words.

Here is an example.

Once while driving down I-35, the rain was coming down really hard and steady, so of course I drove slower than I would have normally driven. In doing so, I happened to be going under a bridge, and I noticed a man, whom I assumed was homeless, trying to shield himself from the rain. It appeared from what I could see in those few moments that maybe this was where he slept. He was frantically trying to put up plastic bags to shield himself from the blowing rain. At that instant, my heart was so heavy because I felt incredible compassion for this situation, and all I could utter were the words "my God." But in doing so, my heart said so much more than that. I was driving, so I could not stop to kneel and pray. But if I am online with God, then the

Holy Spirit is able to take what is in my heart that I am unable to put into words to the Lord as prayers. My heart was heavy in this instance because the Holy Spirit was leading me to pray.

When we are in agreement with the Holy Spirit and online with God, we are praying continuously. The heart of the attitude of praying without ceasing means an ever-open heart to the Lord's leading.

III

What Is Our Motive for Praying?

No doubt as a child, you prayed because your parents wanted you to. In most instances, your parents taught you to kneel and pray at bedtime and to say grace at each meal, so as children, we learned to recite these words over and over. In my case, I was taught to kneel and say my bedtime prayer: "Now I lay me down to sleep, I pray the Lord my soul to keep…" I remember once I knew all the words to this prayer, I would say it each night on my own. However, looking back, I believe I said it out of fear, not because my mother was there beside me making sure that I said it correctly or because I would be in trouble if I did not say it, but because a part of the prayer says, "If I should die before I awake." Die! Did my parents know something I didn't know? Was I going to die? I'm six, so why would I die before I awake? Well, one thing is for sure: that was motivation. I knew at six that I did not want to die before I awoke.

Then I grew older. I was taught the Lord's Prayer. That's very important; you must learn to recite the Lord's Prayer, and I was very happy when I knew all the words and could recite it without making a mistake. But what does it mean to recite something? It means to be able to repeat it from memory, but no one stopped to teach me what all the words meant. I could recite the Lord's Prayer, but I could not tell you what "trespasses" meant. And when I found out that I could ask God for things, I prayed for all kinds of things, all of them selfish.

We must be careful when teaching our children to pray. When we are teaching them the words to the prayers, children must also be taught the motivation of prayer. If left to themselves to figure it out, they will no doubt, as I did, pray for selfish things. Motivation is important because when they don't get that thing that they prayed for at Christmas or for birthdays or when a loved one dies that they prayed for, this can lead to disappointment.

If children grow up feeling as though they had a lack of positive answers to their prayers because maybe as a young child they prayed for Mommy and Daddy to get back together after a divorce and if they don't truly understand the motivation for prayer, by the time they are young adults, this could lead them to resent God or feel as though God is not listening to their prayers, so why pray? The motivation behind prayer is equally as important as the prayer itself. As we mature and grow up, we learn that praying for others helps us take our eyes off our own situations. As we grow in the knowledge of God, our prayers are less self-oriented.

As I thought about my childhood bedtime prayer, I tried to imagine what would have happened if my parents had changed two simple words in my bedtime prayer. What if they had changed that traditional childhood bedtime prayer?

> "Now I lay me down to sleep, I pray the Lord, my soul, to keep. If I should die before I awake. I pray the Lord, my soul to take."
>
> To:
>
> "Now as _we_ lay down to sleep, I pray the Lord, _our_ souls to keep. If _we_ should die before _we_ awake, I pray the Lord, _our_ souls to take."

My bedtime prayers would have instantly become less self-oriented. By changing just those few words, I would have now prayed for all the souls in my home.

What is the correct age to start teaching our children the motivation of prayer and the different types if prayer?

When do children reach an age wherein we are ready to teach them to pray? We have to consider this as parents. I am certain that like me, many of us take our children to church from a very early age, so they sometimes learn how to pray through tradition and routine, sometimes without truly understanding prayer or the motivation behind their prayer.

IV
The Types of Prayer

Intercessory Prayer: act of praying for others

The biblical background for understanding intercessory prayer is found in the Old Testament. The responsibility of the Levitical priest was to stand before and between. We have all heard the stories. Once a year the high priest would enter into the tabernacle; this was known as the Day of Atonement. He would enter into the tabernacle through the first veil, and there he would stop and reflect at the golden lampstand, which held seven candles, and then he would proceed to the table of shewbread (unleavened cakes). He would partake of the shewbread with bitter herbs, and then he would move on to the altar of incense and burn incense to the Lord. Once that was done, only the high priest, carrying blood with him to make atonement for our sins, could enter through the "veil" and into the Holy of Holies. Legend has it that before the high priest could enter the Holy of Holies, a rope was tied around his ankle because if God found that he had not made the proper atonement for his sins before appearing before Him, he would drop dead and his body pulled out from behind the veil with the rope.

The veil was made of fine linen; its colors were blue, purple, and scarlet yarn. There were figures of cherubim (angels) embroidered onto it. Cherubim are spirits who serve God; they demonstrate His almighty power and majesty. They also guard the throne of God.

The word "veil" in Hebrew means a screen, divider, or separator that hides. What was this curtain hiding? Essentially, it was shielding a Holy God from sinful humanity. Whoever entered into the Holy of Holies was entering into the very presence of God. In fact, anyone except the high priest who entered into the Holy of Holies would die.

In the Old Testament, this is an example of intercession. The priest entered into the Holy of Holies, and his job was to intercede on our behalf. He stood before God to offer prayers and sacrifices for our sins, and he stood between God and the people.

The high priest was God's chosen mediator.

In the New Testament, we find that the veil has been torn.

The veil in the temple was a constant reminder that sin renders humanity unfit for the presence of God. The veil was symbolic of Christ Himself as the only way to the Father (John 14:6). This is indicated by the fact that the high priest had to enter the Holy of Holies through the veil.

Although there is an uncertainty as to the exact measurements of a cubit, it is safe to assume that this veil was somewhere near sixty feet high and four inches thick. It was said that horses tied to each side could not pull the veil apart.

When Jesus cried out from the cross, "It is finished," at that moment the veil of the temple was torn in half from top to bottom.

So what significance does this torn veil have for us today?

When God ripped the veil from top to bottom, God was saying, "You no longer are on the outside. You can come in. My Son has made a way for you."

The tearing of the veil was not so much about God no longer residing in the tabernacle (He was never contained there, as it were) but merely the revelation that you and I no longer need the high priest to meet God for us. We have access to God through His Son Christ Jesus.

John 14:6 says, "I am the way, the truth, and the life, no man cometh to Father, except by me."

Jesus is our intercessor. He stands between humankind and God.

Most of us have heard the phrase "standing in the gap." When we enter into intercessory prayer, we are standing in the gap for someone else.

Jesus Christ is our model for intercessory prayer.

Many still believe that because God needs people He can talk to, people who will listen to Him, people who will discern His will, His word, His spirit, and people who would be sensitive to the material and spiritual needs of the world, intercessory prayer can only be performed by a priest. However, the very fact that the veil was torn challenges this theory.

The basis for all prayer is a deep trust in Jesus promise that God hears and answers each prayer. This is a requirement for all Christians, not just the priest.

Consider this.

Someone you love or care for is stricken with cancer. Because of the illness or treatment for the illness, he or she is incapacitated. Or perhaps your loved one is an atheist who turns away every time you try to share Christ with him or her; maybe he or she is angry with God. No doubt every time you turn on the news, you hear of some evil thing that has happened. What can you do? So often, the problems we face seem too big for us. No matter how much we try, we cannot solve them on our own. It's times like these when we need to turn to the Lord in prayer.

Intercessory prayer is a prayer that pleads for the needs of others to be met. "Intercession is warfare." It is the key to God's battle plan, but the battleground is not of this earth. The Bible tells us in Ephesians 6:12, "For we, wrestle not against flesh and blood, but against principalities, against powers, against the rulers of the darkness of this world, against spiritual wickedness in high places."

Intercessory prayer is one of the most potent forces known to humanity. 1 John 4:4 states, "For we, have been made partakers in Jesus victory over sin and death."

2 Corinthians 10:3–4 says that in prayers, we have a weapon that has "divine" power to destroy strongholds.

Intercessory prayer is a serious matter, and just like soldiers who are preparing for battle, we cannot take on the enemy if we leave our weapons behind. That's why we must go into "battle" armed for spiritual conflict.

First, recognize that Jesus is in control of the situation. Jesus rules over forces, authorities, power, and rulers—over all beings in this world and future worlds as well (Eph. 1:21).

We must consider seven steps before going into intercessory prayer.

1. Since the prayer of the righteous is powerful and effective (James 5:16), examine your conscience before you pray and repent of any sin or harsh feelings you may have against other people.
2. Spend a few minutes in silence to quiet your mind and come into God's presence.
3. During this time, ask the Lord to give you a sense of the things God wants you to pray for. Put aside your own agenda, concerns, and desires and unite yourself with Jesus's heart. You may want to write down the things that God places on your heart.
4. Briefly reflect on what you wrote down. What do you think God is leading you to pray for?
5. Pray for the things on God's heart—for those who have no faith; for those who have fallen away from Jesus; for renewal and unity in all churches; for respect for all life; for all the lost, abandoned, or forgotten children of the world; for those under the power of addictions or bound by depression, anxiety, or bitterness; and for prisoners and service men and women. And, of course, pray for your own intentions and those of your loved ones.
6. As you pray, take confidence in God's power to overcome any obstacle. Stand firm in faith and wait to see God work in power.
7. In your prayer journal, keep a record of what you prayed for and of the ways God answered those prayers. Thank and praise Him for all the ways He has worked through your prayer.

Intercessory prayer is a prayer that doesn't give up. This kind of prayer endures all setbacks and overcomes every obstacle. It's prayer that "presses on" until we "apprehend" God's will in whatever situation we are praying for.

Petitionary prayer: supplication, wherein one party humbly or earnestly asks that something be provided either for the party who is doing the supplicating or in some ways can be considered intercessory prayer on behalf of someone else.

When researching petitionary prayer, I realized that for many, this is a very touchy subject, by far one of the most controversial.

The argument:

If as a Christian, you believe that God is omniscient—having complete or unlimited knowledge, awareness, or understanding; perceiving all things; and every decision that He makes is in light of all the facts—then there cannot arise any new information that God failed to take into account. That means that God is fully aware of both our needs and our desires. God is sovereign; whatever God is going to do, He will do; what He is not going to do, He won't. So why waste our time with petitionary prayers for things God already knows we need or want?

Think about it. I have prayed for God to remove all 232 blackheads on my body. God knows that there are exactly 326 blackheads. OK, so maybe my numbers are a little off, but the point is, He knows, so why won't He just fix it?

Some would have you to believe that because God does not just automatically fix things, there is no God.

But let's examine this a little differently. Let's look at what Jesus says regarding petitionary prayer: "Therefore, I tell you, whatever you ask for in prayer, believe that you have received it, and it will be yours" (Mark 11:24).

As Christians, we see this as a promise because we know and believe God cannot lie, and He cannot fail.

It becomes a problem when it looks as if the promise isn't true. I have asked and believed, but I have not received, so there must be something wrong with the teachings of Jesus or there is something wrong with me.

Maybe I am misunderstanding Jesus's promises on prayer. Let's look at it again: "Whatever you ask in My name I will do it, that the Father may be glorified in the Son."

Here, we realize for the first time a vital condition of prayer or a qualifier. "In My name" means in full consciousness that He is the element in which prayer activity lives and moves.

"That I will do": He does not say that He will be a mediator or an advocate with God that it might be done. He declares that He will do it Himself, which is proof of His deity and omnipotence.

I think that if we are going to understand the promise, we must discuss the qualifiers. If we look elsewhere in the Bible, we find the following scripture: "Whatever you ask in my name, I will do it, that the Father may be glorified in the Son; if you ask anything in my name, I will do it" (John 14:13).

In Jesus's name is the first qualifier. What does it mean to ask in the name of Jesus?

We are taught to end our prayers in the name of Jesus, and all of us when praying do this in some form or another. But do we know why? Is it just referring to a way to close out our prayers?

First, let's establish that it is scriptural to pray in the name of Jesus. John 14:13–14, John 15:16, and John 16:23–24, 26 all tell us to pray in the name of Jesus, but is this just a formula or is there more to it?

In order to understand praying in Jesus's name, we must understand (1) the biblical concept of a name, (2) the importance of God's name, and (3) what it means to act in someone else's name.

> Proverbs 22:1: "A good name is rather to be chosen than great riches and loving favor rather than silver and gold."

> Ecclesiastes 7:1: "A good name is better than precious ointment; and the day of death than the day of one's birth."

There is extraordinary value in a good name. Besides a person's soul, this is the most important possession he or she has. A person's personality, character, reputation, authority, virtue, and integrity are all wrapped up in his or her name.

Doing something in someone else's name has two implications. First, you come by the authority of the other person. You are not coming from your own authority but because someone else authorized you to take action. When David fought Goliath, he came unto him "in the name of the LORD of host," the God of the armies of Israel (1 Sam. 17:45). He was not coming in his own power or authority but in that which belonged to God alone. This gave David the authority and ability to defeat Goliath. Second, when you come in someone's name, you come in his or her stead. The person to whom you come is expected to react to you not on the basis of who you are but as if the person who sent you was there him- or herself.

Let's apply this to praying in the name of Jesus. First, it means that when we come to the Father, we come because Jesus sent us. Second, the Father is obligated to treat us as He would His own Son because we come in His stead. I know there are some of you that say this is too much to take in, so consider these verses:

Ephesians 1:5–6: "Having predestinated us unto the adoption of children of Jesus Christ to Himself, according to the good pleasure of His will. To the praise of the glory of His grace, wherein He hath made us accepted in the beloved."

Romans 8:17: "And if children, then heirs; heirs of God, and joint-heirs with Christ; if so be that we suffer with Him, then we may be also glorified together."

How glorious it is to be adopted into the family of God as children because we are heirs with Jesus Christ; we share in the same inheritance. The Father looks upon the redeemed as if He were looking on His Son Jesus Christ. When we pray in the name of Jesus, we know we are unworthy of receiving anything from God. The only reason God should grant our request is that we come in Jesus's name. It is not a magic formula but a heart attitude.

It is important for us to remember that we should always pray in the name of Jesus; however, we should also know that the phrase "in the name of Jesus" also requires the right heart attitude. At our best, we are but filthy rags; therefore, who we are makes no difference, but coming in the name of Jesus has authority. That is power! We, however, must remember that this is not a secret mystery or magical way to get our way with God. This is simply a reminder that the right we have to approach God is through the shed blood of Jesus Christ. Many have had the attitude of humility and trust without the formula "In Jesus's name." We must be careful; oftentimes many use the right formula without having the right attitude.

Our second qualifier is "that the Father may be glorified in the Son." Jesus says in John 5:30, "I can of mine own self do nothing, as I hear, I judge, My judgment is just because I seek not mine own will; but the will of the Father, which hath sent me." As Christians, this must be the essential element of our petitions. The glory of the Father must be the aim and end, the very soul and life of our prayer. Jesus, in His promise of an answer to our prayers, makes this His first objective: the glory of His Father. Is it so with us? Or are in large measure self-interest and self-will the strongest motives urging us to pray? When we begin to understand that, the desire for the glory of the Father is not something we can summon up and present to our Lord when we prepare ourselves to pray. Only when the whole life, in all its parts, is given up to Gods glory can we really pray to His glory. "Do all to the glory of God" and "Ask all to the glory of God." These twin commands are inseparable; obedience to the former is the secret to grace for the latter. A life to the glory of God is the condition of the prayers that Jesus can answer "that the Father may be glorified."

What a humbling thought. So often, there is an earnest prayer for a child, friend, coworker, or someone in our circle. However, the thought of our own joy or pleasure is far stronger than any yearning for God's glory. It's no wonder that there are so many unanswered prayers, yet here we have the secret. God would not be glorified when that glory was not our objective. In order to pray the prayer of faith, we have to give ourselves over literally so that the Father in all things may be glorified in Him. This must be our aim; without this, there cannot be prayer of faith. "How can ye believe," said Jesus, "which receive honor of one another, and not seek the honor that cometh from God only" (John 5:44). That we must surrender to God and seek His glory, with the expectation that He will show His glory in hearing us, are at the root one. He or she that seeks God's glory will see it in the answer to his or her prayer and him or her alone.

In death, Jesus glorified Him; through death, He was glorified with Him. As the redeemed, it is by dying, being dead to self, and living for God that we can glorify Him. This death to self, this life to the glory of God is what Jesus gives to each one of us who can trust Him for it. Jesus places a surety (guarantor, sponsor) within us. The Holy Spirit is given, waiting to make it our experience if we only trust and let Him. What peace and power there will be in our prayers. We will then know ourselves through His grace, in perfect harmony with Him who says to us and promises to do what we ask: "That the Father may be glorified in the Son."

Praise prayer: a prayer of praise that is all about God

We ask nothing; we focus on nothing but God Himself.

Many consider praise prayer the highest form of prayer, so why don't we praise God more often? One reason is that it's not something that comes naturally; we have to learn to praise. Most of us as children learned how to ask for things on our own, but we needed help when learning to say things like "Thank you" or "God, you are awesome." Even after we learned these things, there are often other things that get in our way for praising God.

Unlike intercessory prayer, when we ask God for something on behalf of someone else, or petitionary prayer, when we ask God for something or to do something for us, praise prayer is about God and God only. At its best, it's completely self-forgetting—the very idea of what it means to be a Christian. Many struggle with the idea that God wants or needs our praise. Believe it or not, many Christians out there secretly wonder about this. However, they are afraid to ask the question for fear that they are thought of as un-spiritual. They find it hard to believe that the Supreme Being would require praise from His creations unless He also had a Supreme Ego.

God is completely self-sufficient; He doesn't need our praise and worship. However, He does deserve it.

There is a sense wherein an attribute, which is an action, is not fully realized until it is enacted. Love isn't real without an object of affection. Forgiveness is ethereal until somebody has crossed you. Being a redeemer requires something or someone to save. God is omnipotent, so it is not that He has a need for recognition. But in there is a sense that He had to have creatures to reveal Himself to in order for all the fullness of His being to be realized. His glory is glorified as it is beheld, even if it is beyond the grasp of the beholder.

C. S. Lewis in *Reflections on the Psalms* states, "The world rings with praise, lovers praising their mistresses, readers their favorite poets or authors, walkers praise the countryside, players praising their favorite game. I have noticed that just as men spontaneously praise whatever they value, they also spontaneously urge us to join them in praising it: Isn't she lovely? Wasn't that glorious? Don't you think that was magnificent? The Psalmist in telling everyone to praise God, we are doing what all men do when they speak of what they love or care about. We delight to praise what we enjoy because the praise not only expresses, but it completes the enjoyment; it is its appointed consummation."

When God tells us to sing and raise our hands to Him, it's because it displays to one another God's greatness, kindness, and love. When I hear you give thanks to God, I am again reminded of His goodness. You display God's glory to me, and it builds my faith; it helps me love and trust Him more. When we do works of love, we display the character of Christ that God is forming in us.

Praising God, acknowledging His goodness, love, perfection, and all the incredible things He has done for us, brings Him pleasure.

Consider this: We all understand the concept of praise being due certain people. Imagine that you composed a beautiful symphony and won a very prestigious award for your composition. But when the time came for the award ceremony, they gave the prize for your composition to the wrong artist. That would not be just, right, or good. In the same way, God, as the only being, perfect in goodness, justice, love, and so on is worthy of our praise. We do in fact owe Him that praise. He wants us to praise Him because it is right and good for us to do so. Beyond praise being right and good, praising and worshiping God also brings us joy; it enhances our relationship with Him.

Psalms 34:1 states, "I will bless the LORD at all times: his praises shall continually be in my mouth."

David writes in the Psalms that he will bless the Lord at all times and that he will not only do this in his heart, but he will do it with his tongue. His praise shall continually be in his mouth so "that others may hear it, that others may begin to praise Him too." What a blessed mouthful! If more people had God's praises in their mouths, they would not so often have time for finding fault with others.

What robs us of our ability to praise God?

Inattention is probably the primary culprit. We get caught up in the daily press of life. Busy executives, fame seekers or the type-A personality, corporate-ladder climbers are not only focused on their careers. It's just as easy to get caught up with family, friends, and even church service. Remember that old saying: "Those the devil can't turn, he makes busy." It's too easy for us to get too busy to notice the really important things, so we miss opportunities to praise. It just doesn't occur to us.

Pride: Pride will stop true praise. It is one of the great stumbling blocks to worship.

Self-will: The ugly twin of pride is self-will. One of the saddest stories in the Bible that deals with self-will is the story of Aaron's two sons, Nadab and Abihu,

They were with Moses and knew Gods Law regarding offerings, yet took it upon themselves to lite the offering in the censers and were thus consumed by the fire.

Tradition: Tradition prompts us to expect things that are irrelevant to God's kingdom. Human tradition expects people to dress and act a certain way at church. But true worship isn't prescribed by tradition; it springs from the heart and is led by the spirit.

Judgment: Tradition brings along his friend judgment. Those adhering to one's traditions are quick to judge and condemn those of another tradition. Even great worshiping churches fall into the traps of tradition and judgment.

A critical spirit: The enemy loves it when people are critical because the trap of a critical spirit will keep a person from becoming a true worshiper. When we judge, condemn, and criticize others, we build a wall that separates us from the presence of God. As long as we are pointing out the weakness of others, we don't have time to allow God to cleanse us from our own.

Ignorance: There is a correct and incorrect way to worship God. When we have heard the truth, there is really no excuse for our ignorance; lacking the spiritual knowledge to "worship in truth" keeps us from true worship.

Unforgiveness: Forgiveness is not optional for the true worshiper. It is a requirement. God won't forgive us if we refuse to forgive others.

Complaining: Complaining provokes God's wrath. It constructs a wall of doubt and mistrust between the presence of God and us. Complaining focuses on a problem or a person instead of on Jesus.

Gossip: Not only does gossip hurt others, but it also distracts one's heart from true worship. In the midst of what should be worship to God, the entrapped gossiper is thinking about what he or she has just heard about another person instead of thinking about what God has just said.

Why is it important to Praise God?
The book of Psalms is the praise book of the Bible, and it gives hundreds of reasons why praise is important. As Christians, we should know that praise is a vital part of the life of surrender to God; it gives credit where credit is due. Psalm 107:8 says, "O that men would praise the Lord for His goodness, for his wonderful works to the children of men." Many people end up praising fallible human beings rather than God; they lack the truth. "They exchange the truth about God for a lie, they worship and served the creature rather than the Creator." Sadly, there are those who do not want to recognize God as their Creator because they do not want to be accountable to Him. As Christians,

we should never compromise by exalting the creation over the Creator. We need to stand firm on the truth of God's Word because this is the very foundation for praising God.

Landmark prayer: A geographical location, marker, or landmark that invokes us to pray

Many of you are old enough to remember *Engel vs. Vitale*, which is the Supreme Court case that ruled against prayer in school on June 25, 1962. While studying and researching, I realized that with the exception of this Supreme Court case, which is known as the Landmark Prayer Case, there is very little written at all about landmark prayer. However, I have found that landmark prayer has become an essential tool in my daily routine and goal to pray without ceasing.

In *Engel vs. Vitale*, the Supreme Court ruled that since there should be a clear separation of church and state, prayer in school was unconstitutional. No matter what side of the argument you find yourself on, I believe we can all agree that as a whole, the world could do with a lot more prayer and a lot less politics.

While it is still considered illegal to pray in school, the use of landmark prayer is not confined to schools. Landmark prayer means to single out locations in your daily commute or routine that you can use as a geographical marker to invoke prayer.

This does not mean that we are to stop at each of these locations and pray. Some of us would never make it to work or school on time if we did. However, in our commute to and from our different destinations, there are certain locations that we pass by every day in our cars, on the bus, or on the train.

I have found that my daily commute to my office is one of the most peaceful times for me. I often find myself talking to God. Many of us already pray or talk to God while we are driving to and from work, home, or school. By incorporating landmark prayer into our daily commute, it allows us to be more online with God. Of course, I am not suggesting that you close your eyes and pray while you are driving; let's be clear that we must always put safety first, but consider the following.

A mother has gotten up, praised the Lord for another day, and loaded up her car with her eight-year old child. She is now headed out on her daily commute. During her commute, she first passes a hospital. She takes advantage of this landmark to say a prayer for the sick. "Father, I come to you today asking that you stop by this hospital (hospitals) all over the land today. I ask that you touch those who are sick, in pain, and having surgery or procedures today Father, bless them in a special way. These things I ask in the name of Jesus. Amen."

She continues on her commute and arrives at her child's school; she has this location marked as the perfect opportunity to pray for her child. "Father, I come to you today asking that you bless Tessa as she enters into the school today. Father, I ask that she is obedient to her teachers and kind to her classmates, Then, Father, I ask that you look in on our children and teachers all over the nation. Father, allow them to learn and thrive in a peaceful, safe environment. These things I ask in the name of Jesus. Amen."

She makes one last stop at the dry cleaners to drop off her husband's shirts before arriving at work. This is a perfect opportunity for her to pray for her husband. "Father, I ask that you bless my husband today and allow his place of work to be a safe, productive environment for him as well as his coworkers. Father, I ask that you grant him traveling grace as he travels to and from on the dangerous highway today. These things I ask in the name of Jesus. Amen."

She has arrived at work, so as she parks her car, she uses this location as an opportunity to pray for herself as well as her coworkers. "Father, I come to you today thanking you for allowing me to arrive at work safely. Father, I thank you for my job. Now, Father, I ask that you be with me today. Father, allow my office to be a safe, productive environment and bless my coworkers today. Father, grant them traveling grace as they travel to and from. These things I ask in the name of Jesus. Amen."

As you can see, her prayers were not long, lofty prayers; however, by utilizing her landmarks, she has accomplished her goal of staying online with God. We must be careful to not allow the stress of our daily commute to stress us to the point that we are no longer online with God. Remember, in order to be online with God, we have to have the right heart attitude; we cannot accomplish this if we fall victim to distractions during our commute, such as phone calls, radio, or road rage.

If we are online with God and learn to use landmark prayer effectively, we will find that our daily commute will be less stressful, and when we arrive at work, church, and different destinations, our overall attitude toward our fellow church members, coworkers, and supervisors will be much more positive.

Imagine that three hundred people pass Methodist Hospital on an hourly basis. Of that three hundred, imagine if 125 of those people have Methodist Hospital set as a landmark prayer location. What a mighty move of God this would be! Imagine the blessing that the Father would bestow upon those who are sick because 125 complete strangers are online with God and are praying in concert because they have that hospital as a landmark for prayer.

V
Understanding the Lord's Prayer

Many of us can recite the Lord's Prayer because we have been taught to do so since we were children. But how many of us can explain what it means?

Jesus did not intend for us to recite the Lord's Prayer as if we were chanting a magical incantation that would force God to do what we want. Jesus gave us the Lord's Prayer to be used as a pattern for His followers to copy. The different parts of the Lord's Prayer are meant to teach us something about God, prayer, and our needs.

<u>King James Version</u>
Our Father which art in heaven:
We should always start our prayers out recognizing that we are praying to God Almighty who is in heaven. We should approach God as a child would approach his or her loving father: respectfully, with humility and love. Starting our prayers out humbly shows that we recognize whom God is and who we are.

Hallowed be Thy name:
If we are honest, the only time we hear the word "hallowed" is when we hear the Lord's Prayer, and even then, many of us don't know what it means.

> *Hallowed:* to make holy, sacred, and consecrated. Our Father acknowledges that He is our Father in heaven. Hallowed acknowledges that

His name is holy. God is not some buddy that we would carelessly address. He is holy, perfect, and different from us.

Thy kingdom come:
The kingdom of God is mentioned sixty-five times in the gospels. The kingdom of heaven is mentioned thirty-one times in Matthew. Jesus said, "I come to preach the good news of the Kingdom of God" (Luke 4:43). This is why He was sent. Well, what is a kingdom? A kingdom is a dome or domain ruled by a king. The kingdom of God is the domain ruled by God. Wherever God has authority is His kingdom.

When we pray "thy kingdom come," we are praying for a domain (world) in which God is king against Satan's kingdom. God is sovereign, and we are declaring that God really is in charge of everything.

Thy will be done on earth, as it is in heaven:
The word "will" means the same as "desire," so by praying for God's will to be done, we are praying for all that God desires to be done. If we pray but refuse to submit to God's authority or will ("your will be done"), then we are only deceiving ourselves, and we are not praying the way Jesus taught His followers to pray. As Jesus's people pray and obey God's will for them, His kingdom is made increasingly evident to the unbelieving world around them. We pray that others and we may be brought into the obedience of all laws and ordinances of God. Let God's will be done so that it will introduce a heaven upon earth.

Give us this day our "daily bread":
God provides. He does not give us everything we ask for, but He gives us everything we need. When we look back at scripture, we find that God, while leading the Israelites out of Egypt, provided manna from heaven each morning for them to eat. God did not give them enough to last any more than a day so that they would have to continue to rely on Him to provide. If we are following Jesus each day, we can trust that He will provide everything we need for today, and He will provide for everything we need tomorrow. God cares for His children and takes care of them.

And forgive us our debts, as we forgive our debtors:
The word "as" in this passage of our prayers is a key and stands as a qualifier to the conditions that we can be forgiven. God is the only one who can forgive us of our sin. When we ask God to forgive us our debts, we are asking God to forgive our sins. What we need to understand is that we are asking God to forgive us of our sins as we forgive others who have sinned against us." So if you have not forgiven everyone who has sinned against you, there is no validity in this petition. Jesus tells us in Matthew 6:14–15, "For if you forgive others when they sin against you, your heavenly Father will also forgive you. But if you do not forgive others their sins, your Father will not forgive your sin." We must remember that if we make an unforgiving spirit a virtue, we cannot be forgiven. The Puritan Thomas Watson once said, "A man can as well go to Hell for not forgiving as for not believing." Charles Spurgeon, in a sermon, once said, "Unless you have forgiven others, you read your own death warrant when you repeat the Lord's Prayer." C. S. Lewis wrote, "No part of [Jesus's] teaching was clearer, and there are no exceptions to it."

And lead us not into temptation but deliver us from evil:
We have asked God to forgive us of our sins. It is important to understand that we must also repent; confessing our sins in prayer is really important. So when we think about repentance, we should think of it as making a U-turn. Imagine you're driving the wrong direction on the highway. You may not be able to see it right away, but there is tragedy up ahead if you do not turn around. That's the way we should see repentance.

When we say, "Lead us not into temptation," let's be clear: It is not as if God tempted anyone to sin. What we are asking is, Lord, do not let Satan loose upon us; bind him, and do not leave us to ourselves because we are weak.

Temptations are to be prayed against. If we do not confess our sins, we are doomed to repeat them. We must be fully dependent upon the Holy Spirit who lives in Christians to give us eyes that see temptation coming and feet to escape it by making the U-turn. Here is an example of praying against temptation that I believe everyone can relate to.

"God, I know that I have sinned by gossiping about my church member. This does not honor you and isn't what you want from me. I want to speak well of people, not be known as a gossip or slanderer. When I am tempted to gossip, remind me of your desire for me to speak well of people and make me a blessing rather than a discouragement."

No need to raise your hand, but I know all of us know a few people like this in our congregation or life. If you don't, well, maybe, just maybe, you are that person. No matter what side we are on, we all have to learn to pray against temptation. We have to ask to recognize when evil and temptation are coming our way so that we can make the U-turn and we can be delivered from it.

For Thine is the kingdom, and the power, and the glory, forever. Amen.
When we are closing out our prayer, we pray for God's kingdom, power, and glory to be lifted up and made more beautiful in the eyes of all people. "Thine is the kingdom" acknowledges that we know God has power over the world. "And the power" acknowledges that He supports and maintains that kingdom. "And the glory" acknowledges all that is given and done according to His riches and glory. "Amen" is an expression that means "so be it" or "make it so." By closing out our prayers with "amen," we are declaring that we truly believe that God has heard everything we have said and that He will do it.

VI
Examples of Prayer

Once while at work, the president of our company called me into his office. Of course, my thoughts were initially, Lord, what did I do? But as it turned out, he called me into his office because his wife was having a prayer breakfast at their home that upcoming weekend, and he wanted me to assist him with learning a prayer. Imagine my surprise; first, the relief of knowing that I was not in trouble but then of course the realization of what an honor it was for someone to ask "teach me to pray." I assured him that everyone can pray and that the important thing is to go into prayer with the right heart attitude, so I provided him with a few really simple prayers to choose from.

It is my hope and prayer that the few simple prayers I provided him assisted him in finding his own words when talking with the Lord.

I have included a few sample prayers in hopes of helping others who may not know where or how to find their own prayer voices.

Sample Intercessory Prayers
Prayer for healing
Lord Jesus, You are the master of life and death.
Everything I have is Yours, and I love You very
Deeply. Just one touch from You restores the sick,
Heals the broken, and transforms the darkness.

Only You can do this, only You.
So I ask that You would be with (name) right now.
May (he or she) sense Your presence,
And may (he or she) know Your love.
May (his or her) body be overwhelmed
With light and truth
And with healing and wellness.
Just as it was in the beginning
As You first intended us to be,
May (he or she) be restored.
I ask for healing on (his or her) body right now.
Thank you, Lord, that You hear my prayer,
That You have overcome the world.
And that You hold all of heaven and earth in Your
Loving hands.
These things I ask in the name of Jesus.
Amen.

Prayer of encouragement for a friend
Oh Lord,
I love this friend so much.
He/she has been so kind to me.
I pray that (he/she) will see (him- or herself) and love (him- or herself) fully.
(He or she) gives out much each day; please fill (him or her) up again
With love from others, humility, restful times, and hope
That never ends.
(He or she) is beautiful both inside and out.
(He or she) is a true rainbow, full of color, fun, and grace.
(He or she) allows (his or her) light to shine for all to see.
Bless (his or her) today and always.
In the name of Jesus.
Amen.

Prayer before an operation
Strengthen Your servant, oh God, to do what (he or she) has to
Do and bear what (he or she) has to bear; that by accepting Your
Healing gifts through the surgeons and nurses, (he or she)
May be restored to usefulness in Your world with a
Thankful heart. These things we ask
In the name of Jesus.
Amen.

Prayer for the unemployed
Lord, we are trusting in You as (name)
Looks for new work.
Lead (him/her) to the right job.
We rest in Your goodness and give You all the praise.
Help (name) as (he or she) seeks to find, apply, and interview for each position.
Father, You know the skills
And the things (he or she) enjoys.
Lord, we ask for more than a wage.
We ask that You watch over (him or her) and (his or her) family in this waiting time.
Help (him or her) to be confident in knowing Your will.
Father, open the right doors for (him or her). Please come and direct (his or her) path.
These things we ask
In the name of Jesus.
Amen.

Prayer for an athlete
Lord, please clear (name)'s head of all distractions
And (his or her) heart of any burdens (he or she) may bear.
Allow (him or her) to perform at (his or her) very best, knowing that You will always be there.

Please lift (him or her) up before the moment so through Your eyes, (he or she) may see and have a clearer understanding as the game unfolds before (him or her).
Father, we ask that with great courage
(He or she) will meet this challenge, as You would have (him or her) to, but keep (him or her) humble and remind (him or her) that (his or her) strength comes from knowing You.
Then, Father, when all eyes are upon (him or her),
At the end of this game, I pray (he or she) will turn (his or her) eyes to You, oh Lord, and to the glory of Your name.
These things we ask in the name of Jesus.
Amen.

Prayer for America
Father in heaven,
We, the people, in the land of the free
And the home of the brave, desperately need You.
Oh that we would leave our ways of seeking to be blessed and instead seek to bless others.
We beg for Your guidance and wisdom
For our leaders.
We ask You to protect our land
From enemies, both without and within,
And we praise You for the freedom
We have through the blood of Your Son.
May Your plan be the desire of our nation.
These things we ask in the name of Jesus.
Amen.

Prayer for faith for others
May the kingdom, power, and the presence
Of the Living God seem nearer to you now more than

Ever before. May your understanding of what you
Possess in Him grow exponentially today.
May you see glimpses of glory everywhere you turn
So you're reminded that God
Is very much at work behind the
Scenes, answering prayers, opening doors,
And moving mountains. Jesus lives to
Pray for you, and when He prays, heaven moves.
Walk full of faith today simply because
Heaven sings a song over you.
God is at work on your behalf,
And any day now, you will see Him break through.
We pray that God blesses you and strengthens
Your faith. These things we ask
In the name of Jesus.
Amen.

Sample Petitionary Prayers
Start of the Morning Prayer

Dear Lord, I give You my hands to do your work. I give You my feet to go Your way. I give You my eyes to see as You see. I give You my tongue to speak Your words. I give You my mind that You may guide my thoughts. I give You my spirit that You may pray in me. Above all, I give You my heart that You may love in me. love the Father, and love all of humankind. I give You my whole self, Lord, so that You may grow in me so that it is You who lives, works, and prays in me. These things I ask in the name of Jesus. Amen.

Prayer for personal renewal and character

Lord Jesus, thank you for bringing me into your family. I want to know you personally May I never disappoint you in the way I treat others. Thank you for dying on the cross for my sins. I open the door of my life and receive You as my Savior and Lord. May others see in me the qualities of character that can only be attributed to Your presence in my life. Thank you for forgiving me of my sins and giving me eternal life. Take control of the throne of my life. Make me the kind of person You would have me to be. Renew a right spirit in me. All the glory and the honor belong to you. These things I ask in the name of Jesus. Amen.

Prayer for when you are fearful
Father God, life seems to be uncertain and out of control. Psalms 121 tells me that you never slumber nor sleep. I know that perfect love casts out fear. You alone, Father, are perfect love, so I call on you, Father, to cast out the fear I feel and replace it with confidence. Father, I know that Your grace is sufficient. So when facing the troubles and evil of this world, Lord, I call on You to take care of me moment by moment, day by day. This I ask in the name of Jesus. Amen.

A prayer of confession
Father God, (I/we) confess that (I/we) have sinned against you in thought, word, and deed, by what (I/we) have done, and by what (I/we) have left undone. Father, (my/our) sins are too heavy to carry, too real to hide, and too deep to undo. (I/we) have not loved you with a whole heart; (I/we) have not loved (my/our) neighbors as (I/we) love (myself/ourselves). Father, please forgive what (my/our) lips tremble to name, what (my/our) hearts can no longer bear, and what becomes for (me/us) a consuming fire of judgment. (I/we) are truly sorry, and (I/we) humbly repent. For the sake of your Son Jesus Christ, have mercy on (me/us), Lord, and forgive (me/us); set (me/us) free from a past that (I/we) cannot change; open to a future in which (I/we) can be changed; and grant (me/us) grace to grow more in Your likeness and image. This (I/we) ask in the name of Jesus. Amen.

Sample Praise Prayers
Holy, holy, worthy, worthy, You are to be lifted up on high, worshiped, and glorified. You are beautiful in all Your ways, pure and righteous, above all others. You are the Lamb of God I choose to worship. You loved me first without reservation, even to the sacrifice on the cross at Calvary. You reach out from

heaven to this earth and willingly draw us to Yourself. You provide all our needs. There is none like you, Lord, and we give you all the praise and all the glory in Jesus's name. Amen.

Father, I give praise to You, who sits on the throne, and to the Lamb of God, for all the praise, all the glory, all the honor, and all the power belong to You. Father, we praise and worship Your name forever and ever. In the name of Jesus. Amen.

Father, great and marvelous are Your deeds, Lord God Almighty, just and true are Your ways, King of Nations. Who will not fear you, Lord, and bring glory to Your name? For You alone are holy. All nations will come and worship before You for You are worthy of all the praise. In the name of Jesus we pray. Amen.

God our Father, we pray that the message of your Son will dwell richly among us, as we teach and admonish one another with the wisdom You give and sing with thankfulness in our hearts to You. And whatever we do, in word or deed, may it be done in the name of Jesus and for His glory. Amen.

Sample Landmark Prayers
Schools
Father, I come to you today asking that you bless Tessa as she enters into the school. Father, I ask that she is obedient to her teachers and kind to her classmates. Then, Father, I ask that you look in on our children and teachers all over the nation. Father, allow them to learn and thrive in a peaceful and safe environment. These things I ask in the name of Jesus. Amen.

Hospitals
Father, I come to you today asking that you stop by this hospital and hospitals all over the land today. I ask that you touch those who are sick, in pain, and

having surgery or procedures today. Father, bless them in a special way. These things I ask in the name of Jesus. Amen.

Work

Father, I come to you today thanking you for allowing me to arrive at work safely. Father, I thank you for my job. Now, Father, I ask that you be with me today. Father, allow my office to be a safe and productive environment, bless my coworkers today, and grant them traveling grace as they travel to and from. These things I ask in the name of Jesus. Amen.

Confessions of a Church Mouse

Prayer Journal

Bre'nae Whiteley

Confessions of a Church Mouse

Prayer Journal

The Purpose of Prayer
Prayer is not a normal part of the life of natural humankind. Some say that a person's life will suffer if he or she does not pray. This is not exactly correct. What actually suffers is the Holy Spirit. When we are born again, the Holy Spirit takes up residence within us. The Holy Spirit is not nourished by food but by prayer. When a person is born again, he or she can either starve or nourish the Holy Spirit. Sadhu Sundar Singh suggests in *At the Master's Feet* that prayer is to "lay hold of God" and that through prayer, we discover the will of God. He writes that we cannot alter the will of God but only come to discover God's will for us.

Journaling, like prayer, can be difficult for some. They feel stressed at the thought of coming up with something to journal about.

> "Do not be anxious about anything, but in everything, by prayer and petition, with thanksgiving, present your request to God." (Phil. 4:6)

Begin journaling during your quiet time; simply write out your thoughts or feelings about the day, the struggles you are going through, and the things that worry you. Use this list to fill in your prayer journal according to the category they fall under. For example, maybe you received a raise today. That is certainly something to jot down under Praise Prayer.

This journal allows us to look at our prayer life as one would a diet. This diet is designed to nourish the Holy Spirit and strengthen our communication with God.

Like all diets, we have to plan our meals as well as our snacks. Now that we understand the types of prayer and the purpose of prayer, let's plan our prayer diet.

A good diet of prayer will consist of the following:

Intercessory prayer: the act of praying for others

Petitionary prayer: a solemn supplication or request to a superior authority; an entreaty

Praise prayer: is all about God. We ask for nothing, we seek nothing, and we focus on nothing but God Himself.

Landmark prayer: a spot or location along your daily route that reminds you to take a moment and talk to God

It is also important to write down or make a note of what God has placed on your heart to pray for. Maybe in casually speaking with someone, he or she asked you to remember him or her in your prayers, or someone had a testimony of something that God did for him or her today. Maybe you noticed something in the paper or on the news that made your heart heavy, and you want to make sure to say a prayer for that person or situation.

Jotting this down in your prayer journal will allow you to be more focused on your prayers, and before you know it, you will find that there is always so much to pray for.

Our Prayer Schedule

6:30 a.m.: meal one: praise prayer
9:00 a.m.: snack: intercessory prayer

11:30 a.m.: meal two: petitionary prayer
1:00 p.m.: snack: praise prayer
2:00 p.m.: meal three: intercessory prayer
5:00 p.m.: meal four: petitionary prayer
8:30 p.m.: snack: praise prayer

Understanding that everyone's schedules are so different, we will find that even when we don't follow our prayer diet strictly, there will always be other opportunities to pray.

One of the ways to accomplish this is to set prayer landmarks for yourself. In other words, if you're driving to work and you pass a school each day on your route, make that school the landmark to offer a prayer. This prayer can be an intercessory prayer for all the children, teachers, and educators in this country. It can be a petitionary prayer, where you ask the Lord to assist your son or daughter with a specific task or issue, or it can just be a praise prayer, thanking the Lord for allowing you to be able to send your child to school today or for your child's safe return home from school the day before. There is no wrong prayer. Landmark prayers can be a very valuable tool in living a prayer-filled life because you alone get to choose the landmarks; be it a school, hospital, doughnut shop, or cemetery, it serves as your reminder to take a moment and talk to God.

Now that we have planned our prayer diet, the last thing that we must do is prep. If we want our diet of prayer to be effective, we must always consider these seven steps before prayer.

1. Since it is the prayer of the righteous that is powerful and effective (James 5:16), examine your conscience before you pray and repent of any sin or harsh feelings you may have against other people.
2. Spend a few minutes in silence to quiet your mind and come into God's presence.
3. During this time, ask the Lord to give you a sense of the things God wants you to pray for. Put aside your own agenda, concerns, and desires and unite yourself to Jesus's heart. You may want to write down the things that God places on your heart.

4. Briefly reflect on what you wrote down. What do you think God is leading you to pray for?
5. Pray for the things on God's heart—for those who have no faith; for those who have fallen away from Jesus; for renewal and unity in all the Christian churches; for respect for all life; for all the lost, abandoned, or forgotten children of the world; for those under the power of addictions or bound by depression, anxiety, or bitterness; and for prisoners and servicemen and -women. And of course, pray for your own intentions and those of your loved ones.
6. As you pray, take confidence in God's power to overcome any obstacle. Stand firm in faith and wait to see God work in power.
7. In your prayer journal, keep a record of what you prayed for and of the ways God answered those prayers. Thank Him and praise Him for all the ways He has worked through your prayer.

Journal Examples:

6:30 a.m. Praise: *thanking God for new day, life, health, strength, job*

9:00 a.m. Intercessory: *Pray for those in authority in the nation, ministers, fellow church members, friends, fellow citizens, the sick, one's enemies, and so on.*

11:30 a.m. Petitionary: *Someone you know is sick, or someone you know has a test or interview. Name that person in prayer, petition God on his or her behalf. Be specific.*

1:00 p.m. Praise: *Thank God for something He has done for someone you know or for a situation or a current event you took to the Lord in prayer.*

4:00 p.m. Intercessory: *Now your day is almost over, and no doubt you have learned of some event in the world that involves someone you work with or at church that you want to pray for.*

7:00 p.m. Petitionary: *Take this time to petition the Lord on your behalf. Petition the Lord for something you want Him to do in your life.*

9:00 p.m. Praise: *Praise God for all He's done for you and your family this day. Give all the praise for this day because He deserves all the praise.*

Testimony:

6:30 a.m. Praise:

9:00 a.m. Intercessory:

11:30 a.m. Petitionary:

1:00 p.m. Praise:

4:00 p.m. Intercessory:

7:00 p.m. Petitionary:

9:00 p.m. Praise:

Testimony:

Philippians 4:6: "Be careful for nothing; but in everything by prayer and supplication with thanksgiving let your request be made known to God."

6:30 a.m. Praise:

9:00 a.m. Intercessory:

11:30 a.m. Petitionary:

1:00 p.m. Praise:

4:00 p.m. Intercessory:

7:00 p.m. Petitionary:

9:00 p.m. Praise:

Testimony:

Mark 11:24: "Therefore I say unto you, What things soever ye desire when ye pray, believe that ye receive(them) and ye shall have (them)."

6:30 a.m. Praise:

9:00 a.m. Intercessory:

11:30 a.m. Petitionary:

1:00 p.m. Praise:

4:00 p.m. Intercessory:

7:00 p.m. Petitionary:

9:00 p.m. Praise:

Testimony:

1 Thessalonians 5:17: "Pray without ceasing."

6:30 a.m. Praise:

9:00 a.m. Intercessory:

11:30 a.m. Petitionary:

1:00 p.m. Praise:

4:00 p.m. Intercessory:

7:00 p.m. Petitionary:

9:00 p.m. Praise:

Testimony:

Matthew 6:7: "But when ye pray, use not vain repetitions as the heathen (do); for they think that they shall be heard from much speaking."

6:30 a.m. Praise:

9:00 a.m. Intercessory:

11:30 a.m. Petitionary:

1:00 p.m. Praise:

4:00 p.m. Intercessory:

7:00 p.m. Petitionary:

9:00 p.m. Praise:

Testimony:

Luke 11:9: "And I say unto you, Ask, and it shall be given you; seek, and ye shall find; knock, and it shall be opened unto you."

6:30 a.m. Praise:

9:00 a.m. Intercessory:

11:30 a.m. Petitionary:

1:00 p.m. Praise:

4:00 p.m. Intercessory:

7:00 p.m. Petitionary:

9:00 p.m. Praise:

Testimony:

Romans 8:26: "Likewise the Spirit also helpeth our infirmities; for we know not what we should pray for as we ought; but the Spirit itself maketh intercession for us with the groanings which cannot be uttered."

6:30 a.m. Praise:

9:00 a.m. Intercessory:

11:30 a.m. Petitionary:

1:00 p.m. Praise:

4:00 p.m. Intercessory:

7:00 p.m. Petitionary:

9:00 p.m. Praise:

Testimony:

Matthew 6:6: "But thou, when thou prayest, enter into thy closet, and when thou hast shut thy door, pray to thy Father which is in secret; and thy Father which seeth in secret shall reward thee openly."

6:30 a.m. Praise:

9:00 a.m. Intercessory:

11:30 a.m. Petitionary:

1:00 p.m. Praise:

4:00 p.m. Intercessory:

7:00 p.m. Petitionary:

9:00 p.m. Praise:

Testimony:

1 Timothy 2:1: "I exhort therefore, that, first of all, supplications, prayers, intercessions (and) giving of thanks, be made for all men."

6:30 a.m. Praise:

9:00 a.m. Intercessory:

11:30 a.m. Petitionary:

1:00 p.m. Praise:

4:00 p.m. Intercessory:

7:00 p.m. Petitionary:

9:00 p.m. Praise:

Testimony:

Matthew 26:41: "Watch and pray, that ye enter not into temptation: the spirit indeed is willing, but the flesh is weak."

6:30 a.m. Praise:

9:00 a.m. Intercessory:

11:30 a.m. Petitionary:

1:00 p.m. Praise:

4:00 p.m. Intercessory:

7:00 p.m. Petitionary:

9:00 p.m. Praise:

Testimony:

James 5:16: "Confess your faults one to another, and pray one for another, that ye may be healed. The effectual fervent prayer of a righteous man availeth much."

6:30 a.m. Praise:

9:00 a.m. Intercessory:

11:30 a.m. Petitionary:

1:00 p.m. Praise:

4:00 p.m. Intercessory:

7:00 p.m. Petitionary:

9:00 p.m. Praise:

Testimony:

Jeremiah 33:3: "Call unto me, and I will answer thee, and shew thee great and mighty things, which thou knowest not."

6:30 a.m. Praise:

9:00 a.m. Intercessory:

11:30 a.m. Petitionary:

1:00 p.m. Praise:

4:00 p.m. Intercessory:

7:00 p.m. Petitionary:

9:00 p.m. Praise:

Testimony:

Ephesians 6:18: "Praying always with all prayer and supplication in the Spirit, and watching thereunto with all perseverance and supplication for all saints."

6:30 a.m. Praise:

9:00 a.m. Intercessory:

11:30 a.m. Petitionary:

1:00 p.m. Praise:

4:00 p.m. Intercessory:

7:00 p.m. Petitionary:

9:00 p.m. Praise:

Testimony:

1 Corinthians 1:4: "I give thanks to my God always for you because of the grace of God that was given you in Christ Jesus."

6:30 a.m. Praise:

9:00 a.m. Intercessory:

11:30 a.m. Petitionary:

1:00 p.m. Praise:

4:00 p.m. Intercessory:

7:00 p.m. Petitionary:

9:00 p.m. Praise:

Testimony:

Philippians 1:3–4: "I thank my God upon every remembrance of you, in all my prayers for you, I always pray with joy."

6:30 a.m. Praise:

9:00 a.m. Intercessory:

11:30 a.m. Petitionary:

1:00 p.m. Praise:

4:00 p.m. Intercessory:

7:00 p.m. Petitionary:

9:00 p.m. Praise:

Testimony:

Colossians 1:3: "We give thanks to God and the Father of our Lord Jesus Christ, praying always for you."

6:30 a.m. Praise:

9:00 a.m. Intercessory:

11:30 a.m. Petitionary:

1:00 p.m. Praise:

4:00 p.m. Intercessory:

7:00 p.m. Petitionary:

9:00 p.m. Praise:

Testimony:

Psalms 66:17: "I cried unto Him with my mouth, and He was extolled with my tongue."

6:30 a.m. Praise:

9:00 a.m. Intercessory:

11:30 a.m. Petitionary:

1:00 p.m. Praise:

4:00 p.m. Intercessory:

7:00 p.m. Petitionary:

9:00 p.m. Praise:

Testimony:

1 Corinthians 14:15: "What am I to do? I will pray with my spirit, but I will pray with my mind also; I will sing praise with my spirit, but I will sing with my mind also."

6:30 a.m. Praise:

9:00 a.m. Intercessory:

11:30 a.m. Petitionary:

1:00 p.m. Praise:

4:00 p.m. Intercessory:

7:00 p.m. Petitionary:

9:00 p.m. Praise:

Testimony:

James 1:6: "But let him ask in faith, with no doubting, for the one who doubts is like a wave of the sea that is driven and tossed by the wind."

6:30 a.m. Praise:

9:00 a.m. Intercessory:

11:30 a.m. Petitionary:

1:00 p.m. Praise:

4:00 p.m. Intercessory:

7:00 p.m. Petitionary:

9:00 p.m. Praise:

Testimony:

Psalms 50:14–5: "Offer to God a sacrifice of thanksgiving, and perform your vows to the Most High, and call upon me in the day of trouble; I will deliver you, and you shall glorify me."

6:30 a.m. Praise:

9:00 a.m. Intercessory:

11:30 a.m. Petitionary:

1:00 p.m. Praise:

4:00 p.m. Intercessory:

7:00 p.m. Petitionary:

9:00 p.m. Praise:

Testimony:

Romans 10:13: "For "everyone who calls on the name of the Lord will be saved."

6:30 a.m. Praise:

9:00 a.m. Intercessory:

11:30 a.m. Petitionary:

1:00 p.m. Praise:

4:00 p.m. Intercessory:

7:00 p.m. Petitionary:

9:00 p.m. Praise:

Testimony:

2 Corinthians 1:11: "You also must help us by prayer, so that many will give thanks on our behalf for the blessing granted us through the prayers of many."

6:30 a.m. Praise:

9:00 a.m. Intercessory:

11:30 a.m. Petitionary:

1:00 p.m. Praise:

4:00 p.m. Intercessory:

7:00 p.m. Petitionary:

9:00 p.m. Praise:

Testimony:

1 Timothy 2:1–2: "First of all, then I urge that supplications, prayers, intercessions, and thanksgivings be made for all people, for kings, and all who are in high positions, that we may lead a peaceful and quiet life, Godly and dignified in every way."

6:30 a.m. Praise:

9:00 a.m. Intercessory:

11:30 a.m. Petitionary:

1:00 p.m. Praise:

4:00 p.m. Intercessory:

7:00 p.m. Petitionary:

9:00 p.m. Praise:

Testimony:

James 5:13–14: "Is anyone among you suffering? Let him pray. Is anyone cheerful? Let him sing praise, is anyone among you sick? Let him call for the elders of the church, and let them pray over him, Anointing him with oil in the name of the Lord."

6:30 a.m. Praise:

9:00 a.m. Intercessory:

11:30 a.m. Petitionary:

1:00 p.m. Praise:

4:00 p.m. Intercessory:

7:00 p.m. Petitionary:

9:00 p.m. Praise:

Testimony:

Matthew 21:22: "And all things, whatsoever ye shall ask in prayer, believing, ye shall receive."

6:30 a.m. Praise:

9:00 a.m. Intercessory:

11:30 a.m. Petitionary:

1:00 p.m. Praise:

4:00 p.m. Intercessory:

7:00 p.m. Petitionary:

9:00 p.m. Praise:

Testimony:

Psalms 40:1: "I waited patiently for the Lord, And He inclined to me and heard my cry."

6:30 a.m. Praise:

9:00 a.m. Intercessory:

11:30 a.m. Petitionary:

1:00 p.m. Praise:

4:00 p.m. Intercessory:

7:00 p.m. Petitionary:

9:00 p.m. Praise:

Testimony:

Acts 1:14: "These all with one mind were continually devoting themselves to prayer, along with the women and Mary the mother of Jesus, and with His brothers."

6:30 a.m. Praise:

9:00 a.m. Intercessory:

11:30 a.m. Petitionary:

1:00 p.m. Praise:

4:00 p.m. Intercessory:

7:00 p.m. Petitionary:

9:00 p.m. Praise:

Testimony:

Romans 12:12: "Rejoicing in hope, persevering in tribulation, devoted to prayer."

6:30 a.m. Praise:

9:00 a.m. Intercessory:

11:30 a.m. Petitionary:

1:00 p.m. Praise:

4:00 p.m. Intercessory:

7:00 p.m. Petitionary:

9:00 p.m. Praise:

Testimony:

Matthew 7:7: "Ask and it will be given unto you, seek, and you will find; knock, and it will be opened unto you."

6:30 a.m. Praise:

9:00 a.m. Intercessory:

11:30 a.m. Petitionary:

1:00 p.m. Praise:

4:00 p.m. Intercessory:

7:00 p.m. Petitionary:

9:00 p.m. Praise:

Testimony:

John 14:13–14: "Whatever you ask in my name, this I will do, that the Father may be glorified in the Son, If you ask me anything in my name, I will do it."

6:30 a.m. Praise:

9:00 a.m. Intercessory:

11:30 a.m. Petitionary:

1:00 p.m. Praise:

4:00 p.m. Intercessory:

7:00 p.m. Petitionary:

9:00 p.m. Praise:

Testimony:

Colossians 4:2: "Continue in prayer, and watchful in the same with thanksgiving."

6:30 a.m. Praise:

9:00 a.m. Intercessory:

11:30 a.m. Petitionary:

1:00 p.m. Praise:

4:00 p.m. Intercessory:

7:00 p.m. Petitionary:

9:00 p.m. Praise:

Testimony:

Jeremiah 29:12: "Then shall ye call upon me, and ye shall go and Pray unto me, and I will hearken unto you."

About the Author

It was not always my dream or ambition to write a book. *Confessions of a Church Mouse* came about after many years of sitting and reflecting on my life's experiences, challenges, victories, defeats, and opportunities, and in all these occasions, there was one common denominator: my faith.

I am a novice writer and a mother of three sons, one of whom was diagnosed twenty-six years ago with autism. I am the daughter and caretaker of a mother who suffers from Alzheimer's and leukemia. Though my life has been filled with challenges, victories, and defeats, if asked, I would tell you that most importantly, I am a woman of faith—faith in God and faith in the power of prayer. I would be the first to tell you that there is no way I could manage the challenges life has brought my way without my faith and prayer. *Confessions of a Church Mouse* is the result of my desire to communicate more effectively with God through prayer. My continued goal is to pray without ceasing!

Recommended Reading

New St. Paul MBC.
Dallas, Texas
Sermons and Teachings Rev. Dr. M. L. Curry. 1999 - Present

Learn the Bible.org.
Sermons By David F. Reagan The Purpose of Prayer

Church Leaders.org.
Rythm of Thanks and Prayer by Mark Altrogge. 06-09-2014

Stand to Reason Blog
Do Our Prayers make a Difference by. Amy Hall Aug. 31, 2011

Sermon Index.net.
Pray without Ceasing by Andrew Murray (1828 - 1917).

Harvest.org
No Longer on the Outside by Greg Laurie Mar 10 2016

Wittenburgtrail.org.
The Lord's Prayer by Rev. Allen Wollenburg.Mar. 7, 2012

Under the Cover of Prayer.wordpress.com
What is our Motive for Praying by Bruce Atchison. July 17, 2013

Miracles Happen when you Pray by. Quin Sherrer. Book pub. 1997

Christlife.org.
The Power of Intercessory Prayer July 15, 2015

The Tabernacle Place.com.
The Holy of Holies and the Veil Lesson 8

The Utmost.Org.
What's the Good of Prayer? By Oswald Chambers

Focus on Prayer.com
Why Pray, Joe Vigliano 2006 - 2012

Leadership Resources.Org
100 Best Charles Spurgeon Quotes by C. H. Spurgeon. Aug. 22, 2014

www.ingramcontent.com/pod-product-compliance
Lightning Source LLC
LaVergne TN
LVHW051509070426
835507LV00022B/3017